IMAGES
of America

DOWNTOWN
SAN ANTONIO

As this man ponders life and the possibility of the future, we look over his shoulder into his past. This view of Alamo Plaza was taken during the 1920s and made from a glass lantern slide for the Keystone View Company. In the center is the Honey Comb rock bandstand and just above the Federal Building and Post Office. (Courtesy of David Peché.)

ON THE COVER: John Wayne leaves the "It's Movietime in Texas, U.S.A." rally during the Council of Motion Picture Organization's promotional tour, which visited the Alamo Plaza in San Antonio, Texas, in 1951. John Wayne, billed the biggest box-office attraction in the world, tipped off his many fans with news of preproduction plans for a saga about the Alamo. Wayne and Mayor Jack White spent part of the day discussing the filming of the picture. (Zintgraff Collection, Institute of Texan Cultures, University of Texas at San Antonio, courtesy of John and Dela White.)

IMAGES
of America

DOWNTOWN
SAN ANTONIO

Joan Marston Korte and David L. Peché
Foreword by Mayor Julián Castro

ARCADIA
PUBLISHING

Published by Arcadia Publishing
Charleston, South Carolina

Library of Congress Control Number: 2012947000

For all general information, please contact Arcadia Publishing:
Telephone 843-853-2070
Fax 843-853-0044
E-mail sales@arcadiapublishing.com
For customer service and orders:
Toll-Free 1-888-313-2665

Visit us on the Internet at www.arcadiapublishing.com

This book is dedicated to Mayor Lila Cockrell in honor of her achievements. At age 90, she continues to serve the city she loves with great passion.

CONTENTS

ACKNOWLEDGMENTS

It was my great fortune that my husband received orders for Kelly Air Force Base while serving in the military as a test pilot. This wasn't just another transfer to another base. It was an eye-opening experience of what was a wonderful city, San Antonio, Texas. Upon his retirement, we couldn't wait to take up permanent residence and raise our children. Upon becoming empty nesters, rather than becoming couch potatoes, we decided to move downtown and involve ourselves in community affairs. Since then, I have become very passionate about the core of my city. I want to thank all the wonderful residents, businessmen and women, city employees, developers, politicians, tourists, visitors, stakeholders, and movers and shakers who have become a part of my life. In speaking out for what my heart tells me is best for our city, I have accumulated many friends. I am very grateful for all of those who have helped me put together this book. I won't mention names for fear of inadvertently leaving someone out. You know who you are, and I thank you from the bottom of my heart. Paula Allen writes a local history column that appears in the *San Antonio Express-News* and is the author of *San Antonio Then and Now*, a book of historical and contemporary photographs of local landmarks. She is the recipient of an Arts and Letters Award from the Friends of the San Antonio Public Library and an award of merit from the San Antonio Historical Association and has been a presenter at a Daughters of the Republic of Texas History Forum. I want to thank her for proofreading this book and lending her expertise when it comes to its accuracy and quality.

—Joan Marston Korte

As a young boy, I started collecting stickers and postcards, and to this day I still have my first collection: NFL team stickers that came on bananas. It is a gene I believe I received from my mom. I love and thank you for everything you've done for me, Mom. Photography was my second passion, which I took after my dad. He took pictures and slides and filmed my family's most cherished moments. I thank and love you, Dad, for instilling in me all of your amazing qualities.

Fast-forwarding in time, I would now like to thank the people who inspired me along the way: Ms. Terry Olivares, my fourth grade teacher at St. James grade school; Native Roberta Ambrosino, my director at the Art Institute of Los Angles, who is now back in San Antonio, where she still offers advice; Norma Cruz-Gonzales, an English teacher at San Antonio College who inspired my creative writing; and my longtime friend Melissa Moore Braddock, whose passion for history and professional insight helped me write the back cover text. I also thank my sister Chris and brother Albert for offering their knowledge of downtown history. Thank you to Mickie Tencza, who offered her writing skill and enthusiasm. Raul E. Medina III has been an invaluable contributor taking photographs for this book. I'm blessed to have met someone who shares the same passion for our city; thank you, my friend.

In early 2010, I was inspired by Mayor Julián Castro's vision of what San Antonio will look like in the year 2020. I joined this call to add my passion for my beloved city and created Downtown San Antonio History. This has been a great journey, and this book is now ready to give back to all those who have come before us but, most of all, to those who now help preserve and create a new Downtown San Antonio.

—David L. Peché

FOREWORD

In my years of public service, one of the things I've enjoyed most is hearing the stories of everyday San Antonians and the reverence they have for our historical downtown.

They remember going down Houston Street to the Majestic Theater, a still beautiful and ornate structure that was the largest of its kind in Texas and the second largest in the country when it was built in 1929. Folks with older memories remember seeing legendary acts like Jack Benny, George Burns, and Bob Hope. That legacy continues today at the Majestic, which hosts the San Antonio Symphony and top-flight Broadway shows.

Longtime residents also fondly recall downtown as a place where they could grab some candy at Russell Stover's near the entrance of the Gunter Hotel and then stroll down the street to marvel at the Christmas window at Frost Bros. Along with the window-shoppers and theatergoers was a steady stream of servicemen on holiday from area military installations.

As a young boy, I remember running with my brother up the stairs of the Aztec Theatre, where I couldn't decide whether to focus on the movie we went to see or the amazing Meso-American architecture.

The downtown of today is certainly different, but it is every bit as unique. The Alamo remains the signature historical tourist attraction in the state of Texas. The River Walk, also known as the Paseo del Rio, is an enchanting 2.5-mile waterway with restaurants, shopping centers, bars, and businesses that are teeming with residents and tourists throughout the day or night.

Downtown remains a crossroads for people of every walk of life. On any given day, parents with children might buy a *raspa*, or snow cone, from a vendor at Main Plaza or Alamo Plaza, while a block away, locals and conventioneers enjoy world-class cuisine at a fine restaurant.

The years pass and new ideas emerge, but the charm of downtown San Antonio remains. Just like the Majestic and the Aztec Theatres, the Milam Building—among the tallest reinforced-concrete buildings in the world and the first to be air-conditioned when it was built in 1928—stands proud among new hotels and office buildings. Far from being an urban jungle, downtown includes a growing number of residents and surrounding neighborhoods like King William, which remind us that new isn't necessarily better and that the center city should be as attractive to San Antonians as it is to tourists.

La Villita, San Antonio's first neighborhood founded by the Spanish on the south banks of the San Antonio River, remains today a vibrant center of art and culture, as well as the annual host to the city's biggest street festival, Fiesta Night in Old San Antonio.

Early in my tenure as mayor, I proclaimed 2010 as the dawn of the "Decade of Downtown." We are off to such a great start, and it is my hope that our continued progress will inspire a new edition of this book in the coming years.

Café College, the city's one-stop college advising center, and the University of Texas at San Antonio (UTSA)'s Downtown Campus anchor the western edge of downtown, exemplifying the importance we as a community are placing on creating a brainpower generation in San Antonio. As that creative class of artists and business professionals continues to grow, the look and feel of downtown is changing.

In addition to an unprecedented effort to plant 1,000 trees downtown, city policies have been changed to emphasize pedestrian and bicycle traffic, including the launch of Texas's first bike-share program, which encourages folks to get out of their vehicles and enjoy downtown on a more personal level.

Inspired local efforts also envision new futures for the San Antonio River to the north and south of downtown and the transformation of the San Antonio Municipal Auditorium into the world-class Bexar County Performing Arts Center. When both projects are finished, the restored ecosystem and the linkages to art and culture on the river will run 13 miles from the San Antonio Museum of Art down to San Antonio's Spanish Colonial missions to the south.

We are also revisiting the site of an event that forever changed the national and global profile of San Antonio and ushered in its modern era: HemisFair 1968. Since that seminal event, HemisFair Park fell victim to benign neglect. But that is changing. The coming relocation of the federal courthouse has spurred a new round of creative thinking that will not only revitalize HemisFair Park but also potentially provide a more reverent gateway to the Shrine of Texas Liberty—the Alamo—and include a more majestic link to the River Walk.

We not only have a chance to carve out a rare spot of urban green space in the heart of the nation's seventh-largest city but also a grand opportunity to create an imaginative mixed-use development that invites more San Antonians to live, work and recreate downtown.

As you will see in the coming pages, the story of downtown San Antonio is a tale of profound history, robust growth, a unique cultural blend and friendly accessibility. Downtown has been, and will continue to be, a gathering place for everyone.

—Mayor Julián Castro

One

MISSIONS AND CHURCHES

The Alamo, located on the northeast corner of Alamo Plaza, is one of the most historic buildings in the world. A stone on the front bears the date 1757, which was probably the year of completion. The mission was originally founded on the banks of the Rio Grande in 1703, and after being twice removed to different sites, it was finally brought to San Antonio, where the cornerstone was laid in 1744. In 1849, Maj. Edwin Babbitt took possession of the Alamo buildings for the Army. He found the Alamo "choked with debris, a conglomeration of stones, mortar and dirt," just as it was left when the twin towers, the dome, and the arched roof fell in (about 1762). As the building was neglected for nearly 100 years, it took him years to entirely clear it out.

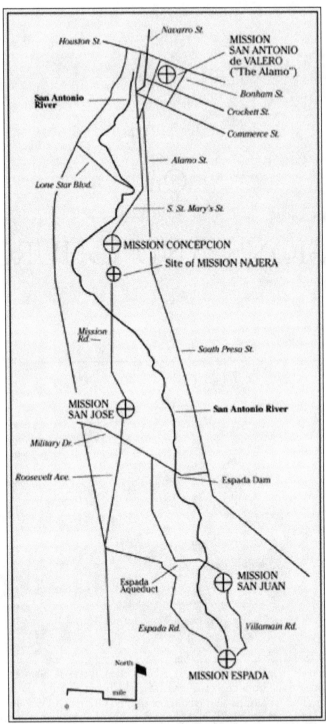

One base for Spanish missionary and military operations in Texas developed around San Antonio. Two missions and a presidio were established in the San Antonio River valley between 1718 and 1720, and the Spanish added three new missions in the valley in 1731. A single presidio protected the five missions, which were closely grouped. (National Park Service.)

Mission Concepcion was built like the others for worship, scholastic purposes, and defense. The barracks that surrounded the square have long since disappeared. The upper part of the ornamented facade is not an arch but a simple triangle, and the arch of the doorway is, for want of a better definition, a divided polygon.

The missions were established as an outreach of the Spanish government and the Catholic Church. The Franciscan Fathers founded each mission to evangelize the regional natives, teach them skills to help them adapt to Spanish ways, and minister to their needs. Additionally, the effort was to make them active citizens of the Spanish province of Texas.

11

Mission San Juan, the third mission, was originally established as San José de los Nazonis in East Texas. In 1731, it was relocated to its permanent home on the east bank of the San Antonio River. By mid-century, San Juan, with its rich farm and pasturelands, was a regional supplier of agricultural produce. In 1762, its herds were reported to include 3,500 sheep and nearly as many cattle.

Mission San Juan, while not as grand or imposing as some of the rest, has served better than the others in providing a general idea of the plan of a complete mission. It featured a walled square, granary, chapel, church, well, fields and gardens, living rooms, cells and offices for the missionaries, quarters, workrooms, and school rooms for the Indian neophytes, kitchens, and refectories. This early-20th-century family could have been descendants of residents of the Spanish Colonial missions.

On March 6, 1836, the story of the Alamo was written in the blood of the bravest of the brave. Fighting for the independence of their country, the immortals fell, and their ashes were mingled with the dust of their beloved homeland. The defenders of the Alamo, whether native-born Tejanos or Texians from the United States or Europe, fought for a Texas independent from Mexico. Crockett, Bowie, Travis, Bonham, and more than 180 obscure heroes fell beneath the persistent onslaughts of Santa Anna and his 6,000 soldiers.

Of all the brave men who died at the Alamo, these four are probably the most notable. James Bowie, a knife fighter, was born in Kentucky in 1796. William Barrett Travis, Commander of the Alamo, was born in 1809 in South Carolina. James Butler Bonham, an American soldier, was born in 1807 in South Carolina. David Crockett, a Tennessee Congressman, was born in Tennessee in 1786.

Mission San Jose de Aguayo, the second mission, is so called in honor of St. Joseph and Governor de Aguayo and is considered by some the most beautiful mission in the United States. It was founded in 1720 and took eight years to build. The facade, especially, is rich in design. Besides Our Lady of Guadalupe there are figures of San Jose, San Benedictine, San Augustine, and San Francisco.

There are several variations of the legend concerning Pedro Huízar's connection with the Rose Window. Most of them contend that as a young man, he was trained as a sculptor in Spain and sailed to the New World to seek his fortune. According to a few of the legends, the Rose Window was so called because the mourning sculptor dedicated it to a lost love named Rosa or Rosita.

While visiting the missions, one can't help notice the beautiful arched walkways around the structures. This is classic Spanish Colonial architecture, mixed with Native American influences and Moorish motifs. Most of the craftsmen were from Mexico, instructed to maintain the Spanish architectural model. The laborers in general were Native American residents who adapted the style to accommodate local weather conditions and materials.

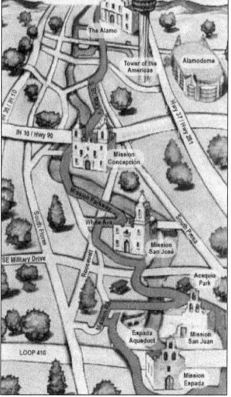

The Old Spanish missions of San Antonio are a chain of five colonial-era compounds located in a southern line from the center of downtown San Antonio to the southern edge of the city. Several gateways provided entrance into the compounds of the walled communities. Bastions, or fortified towers, were located along the walls to provide defense. Living quarters were built inside against the compound walls for the Indian neophytes and Spanish soldiers, usually only one or two of whom would bring their families with them. The church was the focal point of the missions.

The First Temple Beth-El congregation was founded in 1874 at the corners of Travis Street and Jefferson. The Jewish community in San Antonio was part of the large immigration of Germans into Texas in the 1850s and 1860s. As the congregation grew, it was necessary to build a new temple. This structure was dedicated on September 18, 1903, on the same site as the original temple by Travis Park following the demolition of the original structure.

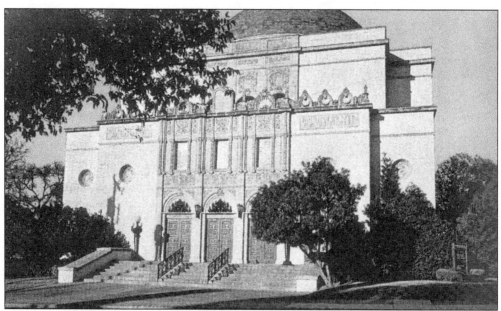

By the mid-1920s, a larger temple was needed, as the Jewish community had grown rapidly as San Antonio itself. This building was dedicated in April 1927; the sanctuary has a 1,200-seat capacity. It continues to serve the Temple Beth-El Congregation (Reform) on Belknap Place just to the north of San Antonio College.

16

In 1882, a lot on the corner of Navarro and Travis Streets was obtained. Travis Park Methodist Church was finally built in 1886. Under the leadership of Rev. John M. Moore, the church grew significantly. The auditorium was enlarged to hold 1,400 members. Large stained-glass windows were added to each side of the altar.

In 1858, worshipers elected a vestry and were admitted to the Diocese of Texas as St. Mark's Episcopal Church, one of 40 churches in the diocese at the time. Once the region recovered from the Civil War, work on Richard Upjohn's Gothic-style limestone building was completed. Lyndon B. Johnson and Lady Bird were married at St. Mark's on November 17, 1934.

St. Mary's Catholic Church was founded to serve the new non-Hispanic immigrants to the area in the mid-19th century. Initially, services were conducted in both English and German. The German population was later served by nearby St. Joseph Church. The initial church on the site was damaged extensively in the flood of 1921 and was replaced with the current building in 1924.

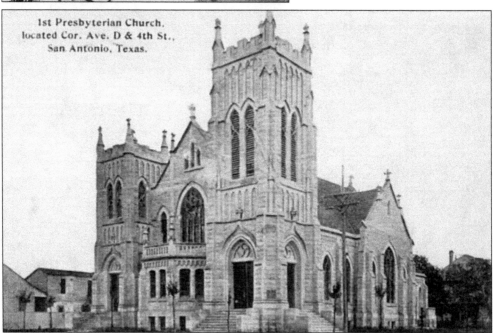

The First Presbyterian Church was forced to move from its location on Main Avenue and Houston Street because the Saturday night revelers from the Buckhorn Saloon across the street became a significant distraction for the Sunday morning worshipers. In 1910, the Gothic stone structure on McCullough Avenue was dedicated. In 1939, the membership grew to over 2,500, making it the largest Presbyterian congregation in the South.

FIRST BAPTIST CHURCH
134 Fifth Street

The First Baptist Church was founded on January 20, 1861, with 13 people and the Reverend John Thurmond in the second floor of a downtown drugstore. The first church was built across from Travis Park, and a spat led the church to split in 1887. The First Baptist Church moved to its current location along the San Antonio River in the early 1900s. Many of its members were from the military community.

During the middle part of the 19th century, thousands of German people in search of peace and freedom came to Texas to find a new home. These sturdy pioneers established the first Lutheran church locally in 1857 under Pastor Phillip Zizelmann. St. John's was built at the corner of South Presa and Nueva Streets. At its peak, St. John's had 3,000 members, making it the largest Lutheran church in Texas.

Grace Lutheran Church began in 1903 to serve Lutherans who wished to worship in English. The beautifully carved altar and impressive stained-glass windows create an inspiring setting for a rich worship experience. From the beginning, Grace has had a legacy of ministering to the needs of the community and has been a leader in a long list of programs and organizations that provide shelter, nourishment, and care.

In 1879, German Methodists constructed this Gothic Revival church in the La Villita area. Little Church of La Villita features pegs carved by a Norwegian sailor. The Methodist church was purchased by the Episcopal Diocese of West Texas in 1895 and by the City of San Antonio in 1945. Today, the church offers worship services and is often the site of weddings.

Evangelist David Pennington came to San Antonio in 1883 and organized this Christian congregation. He held worship services in a variety of borrowed facilities until a sanctuary was constructed at this site in 1884. The Central Christian Church was established during a period of great growth in San Antonio due to the coming of the railroad in 1877, and church membership grew as well.

The engraved sign and the marble sarcophagus said to entomb the ashes of Davy Crockett, James Bowie, William B. Travis, and their comrades tell the visitor that not only is Texas history entombed here but also that San Fernando Cathedral has been and continues to be a part of the state's pride.

The Spanish immigrants from the Canary Islands who picked the spot for the church in 1731 did so with the intention of making it the soul and center of the city. Just outside San Fernando's entrance, there is a plaque stating that the remains of the defenders of the Alamo are buried inside. In 1836, during the 12-day siege, 187 Texas volunteers were killed by some 6,000 Mexican troops lead by Gen. Antonio Lopez de Santa Anna, who ordered their bodies burned. Three walls of the original church still stand, and the cathedral's crypt contains the earliest marked graves in the city. San Fernando has undergone a number of restorations. The latest—in 2002—exposed the original limestone of 1738 and the original floor, three feet below the present floor. These discoveries, as well as charred beams from the fire of 1828 that destroyed much of the colonial church, are on display.

Two

PLAZAS AND PARKS

This view looks south at Alamo Plaza in 1898. Note the Hotel Alamo and Café Bismarch on the right. The rails for the electric trolleys are evident. The building on the left, owned by Hugo Schmeltzer & Co., became part of the Alamo grounds after being purchased and donated by Clara Driscoll.

This photograph was taken of Military Plaza, located behind the San Fernando Cathedral, where it was common for farmers to bring their produce for sale in the middle 1880s. The Spanish Governor's Palace still remains there as a link to the past. The plaza has had a long history as the seat of government. Moses Austin came here in 1820 seeking permission from the Spanish governor to settle Anglo-American colonists in Texas. Construction of the present city hall in the center of the plaza in 1888–1891 put an end to the open-air market, the "'Chili Queens," and the rowdy activities of the cowboys, cattlemen, and gamblers who frequented the plaza outside the old Spanish Governor's Palace and Bat Cave jailhouse.

After the original bandstand was moved to San Pedro Park, Billy Reuter built this new bandstand with a flat roof. He owned a bar across the street on the corner of Crockett Street and Alamo Plaza and sponsored band concerts for his customers in the plaza. The bandstand contained restrooms and a first aid station.

This photograph was taken from the Medical Arts Building, now the Emily Morgan Hotel, in the 1930s. To the left, in the foreground, is the Alamo and its grounds. Further back on the same side is the Menger Hotel. It should be noted that although the parklike property is referred to as Alamo Plaza, it is actually two separate plazas. The property in the foreground with the gazebo is Alamo Plaza. The property in the background, in front of the Menger, is Plaza de Valero.

Pompeo Coppini sculpted *The Spirit of Sacrifice Cenotaph* in 1939. The marker reads, "Erected in memory of the Heroes who sacrificed their lives at the Alamo on March 6, 1836 in the defense of Texas. They chose never to surrender nor retreat, these brave hearts with flag still proudly waving perished in the flames of immortality that their high sacrifice might lead to the founding on this Texas."

In 1912, the Alamo Heroes Monument Association had an architectural drawing prepared to use in the fundraising process. The association wanted the monument to stand 802 feet tall, making it the tallest man-made object in the nation and the second highest in the world at the time. Only the Eiffel Tower, built in 1889, would be taller. The association was unable to raise enough money.

Here is a view of the plaza from the east looking west. San Fernando, once merely a parish church, became a cathedral when the first bishop of San Antonio was installed there on Christmas Eve, 1874. Note city hall behind the cathedral in Military Plaza. To the left are a merchandise store and a barbershop.

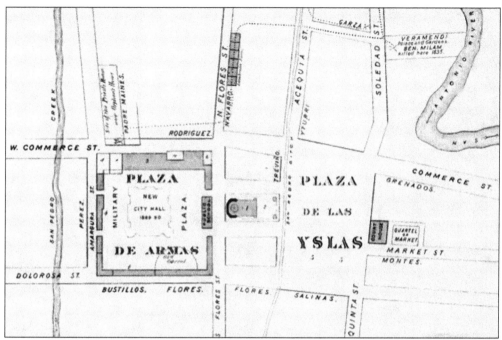

To the east of Main Plaza is the old courthouse, also known as the Bat Cave after the colony of bats that inhabited the structure. Men had to enter the courthouse with big poles to clear out the bats before business could be conducted. The Presidio Garrison Barracks can be seen along the Commerce Street side of Military Plaza. Women used to come and feed the soldiers in the open-air plaza. After the garrison moved out, the first chili stands were set up, and the legendary "chili queens" made their appearance.

A busy market, it teemed with noisy vendors of vegetables, fresh eggs, chili peppers, and live chickens. Oxcarts and wagons stood bulging with hay, hides, and wood. Strolling guitarists, tourists, and girls selling songbirds mingled with pickpockets and other characters. Cockfights were frequently held.

The 1900 photograph is looking south on Soledad Street towards the Bexar County Courthouse. On the right is Main Plaza, lush and shady. To the left is a variety of merchandise shops. The streets are unpaved, and automobiles are noticeably absent.

George W. Brackenridge built an elegant house on the property at the headwaters of the San Antonio River after acquiring it from Mayor James Sweet. It was the showplace of Texas, and he entertained many distinguished guests. The 325 acres were gifted to the city upon his death. The property was known as "the Head of the River."

The San Antonio River meanders by paved, tree-lined paths suitable for walking or bicycling in Brackenridge Park. Additional recreational activities include nature study, birding, fishing, pedal boating, and picnicking. Other facilities include a miniature railroad that ran around the park, a playground, concessions, athletic fields, a golf course, a Japanese tea garden, a zoo, and a museum.

Located in Brackenridge Park, the Municipal Golf Course opened in 1916 as an 18-hole championship course. In 1922, the Texas Open Golf Tournament originated on this course, and it was played here until 1959. The course was totally renovated in 2008. It is a par 71 and measures 6,263 yards from the championship tees.

The Sunken Garden is a registered Texas historical landmark. Alamo Roman and Portland Cement Company, later called Alamo Cement Company, used the quarry from 1880 until 1908, when it moved to a new facility with rail access north of the city limits. Built in the early 20th century, the Sunken Garden transformed the abandoned limestone quarry into a lush year-round garden and floral display featuring shaded walkways, stone bridges, a 60-foot waterfall, and attractive ponds in Brackenridge Park.

The San Antonio Zoo is ranked as one of the best zoos in the nation, exhibiting over 3,500 animals of 600 species. The zoo originally started with a small collection of animals in the 1800s in San Pedro Park. In 1914, George W. Brackenridge began to add deer, monkeys, elk, buffalo, bears, and a couple of lions. The zoo now encompasses 35 landscaped acres. The Richard Friedrich Aquarium was dedicated in 1948, and the Hixon Bird House, funded through the efforts of Col. Frederick C. Hixon, opened in 1966. The zoo's bird collection is now one of the world's largest.

Greetings from San Antonio, Texas. Alamo Plaza. *San Antonio Tex. 8/31/07 Beat Dreyer a game of hand ball for me*

Note the carriages and drivers awaiting fares. Hugo and Schmeltzer's building can be seen in front of the old post office. Clara Driscoll was instrumental in acquiring the building in 1903, when it was put up for sale, so the DeZavala chapter of the Daughters of the Republic of Texas could add it to the chapel in order to begin the proper preservation of the Shrine of Texas Liberty.

SAN ANTONIO, TEXAS. SAN PEDRO SPRINGS.

It was around these lovely springs, under the spreading live oaks and stately pecans, that the Indians struck their tepees, and it was here that Canary Island settlers camped on that November day in 1730 when they first reached San Antonio de Bexar. All of the land included in this park was a part of the original royal Spanish grant in 1729 and has always been for public use.

The Victorian bandstand was moved from Alamo Plaza to the San Pedro Park in 1897. It was placed over the old limestone bear pit. Though in need of repair in 2002, almost all of the bandstand's original form and materials still remain. It did receive a new flat-seamed roof sized to replicate the original historical pattern.

San Pedro Park is the oldest in San Antonio and second only to Boston Common in the nation. Within it boundaries, some of the most stirring events in the history of the city have taken place. A major renovation began in 1915. A swimming pool was built in the old lake bed, and tennis courts, a library, and a community theater were constructed.

The area including Travis Park was once part of the upper farmlands of the Alamo. Samuel A. Maverick bought the property in 1851. He lived at the northwest corner of Alamo Plaza and used it for his orchard. After Maverick died in 1870, the land was deeded to the city. An 1873 map calls the square Travis Plaza, named for Col. William Barrett Travis.

The park is the third oldest in the nation. The house that appears on park property is unidentified, but it might have been the one built by Sam Maverick. Since 1982, the park has hosted a jazz festival called Jazz'SAlive, one of the largest outdoor festivals in the country.

Travis Park, San Antonio, Tex.

THE OLD CANNON THAT WAS USED IN 1836, NOW IN TRAVIS PARK, SAN ANTONIO, TEXAS.

There are two cannons, both on caissons, on display in Travis Park. They are placed to the right and left of the Confederate Civil War Monument. Both cannons appear to be made of bronze or brass and are in good condition. This park is one of the older parks in San Antonio and has the distinction of having had the first dedicated monument in the city placed in it.

In the center of this park, a 40-foot granite shaft rises up from its base to hold a Confederate soldier as a monument to "Our Confederate Dead," as inscribed on the base. The Confederate Civil War Monument was purchased and built through the efforts of the Barnard E. Bee chapter of the Daughters of the Confederacy in 1899.

34

Three

MILITARY AND GOVERNMENT

Gen. David Twiggs, who had a distinguished record of military service with the United States, surrendered the Federal arsenal at the Alamo to the Confederacy on February 16, 1861. After city companies took possession of the Alamo, General Twiggs, accompanied by Maj. William A. Nichols, met Gen. Benjamin McCulloch in the Main Plaza. The horsemen paraded around them, and there was a burst of cheers as the three officers met.

Towards the end of the 19th century, the colony of Cuba began fighting for independence from Spain. When Spain declared war on the United States on April 23, 1898, Theodore Roosevelt, who was then assistant secretary of the Navy, asked permission to start a regiment that would go to Cuba to fight the Spanish. Roosevelt came to San Antonio to recruit and train men for the 1st US Volunteer Cavalry, which came to be known as the Rough Riders.

Pres. Theodore Roosevelt is surrounded by former officers of the Rough Riders regiment and Lt. Gen. Adna Chaffee. Roosevelt had the rank of lieutenant colonel while in San Antonio and throughout his involvement with the 1st Voluntary Cavalry Regiment, better known as the Rough Riders. This picture was taken on April 7, 1905, at a reunion on the International Fair Grounds.

As a second lieutenant and fresh out of West Point, Dwight David "Ike" Eisenhower was assigned to the 19th Infantry at Fort Sam Houston, San Antonio, on September 13, 1915. He met Mamie Dowd at the officers' mess and courted her with Mexican dinners on San Antonio's West Side and dancing on the roof of the St. Anthony Hotel. Ike was serving his second tour at Fort Sam Houston, as brigadier general, when the Japanese attacked Pearl Harbor. He was transferred to the War Plans Division, US Army Staff, under Gen. George C. Marshall. From that time to 1961, he held one responsible position after another. As supreme commander of the Allied Expeditionary Force, he gave the order that sent British and American troops into Normandy on June 6, 1944, also known as D-Day. Eleven months later, on Victory in Europe Day, he accepted the surrender of Nazi representatives Wilhelm Keitel and Alfred Jodl.

Fort Sam Houston was designated as a National Historic Landmark in 1975. As one of the Army's oldest installations and now part of Joint Base San Antonio, Fort Sam Houston boasts the largest collection of historic structures among US bases—more than 900 buildings. Even more consequential than the numbers is the historical integrity of the post's different sections that represent different eras of construction. Careful preservation of these areas allows the post to live with its history, surrounded by the traditions of excellence established when the first soldier arrived here in 1845.

During World War I, approximately 1,280 acres northwest of Fort Sam Houston were added and called Camp Travis. These two Army servicemen are seen on spotlight duty.

The YMCA was located at 217 Avenue E. The staff looked after the comfort and welfare of the men from the Army and Navy. It was reported that more than a quarter million men made use of this building.

Pictured are (1) soldiers asleep on the roof of the Elks Club Building, (2) cots on the lawn, (3) soldiers lined up in the coffee shop, (4) L.G. Williamson, executive secretary, and (5) government trucks manned by the US Army.

Seen here are (1) men of 2nd Division trains who proved heroes in the floodwaters of 1921, (2) Medical Corps who tended to the sick and injured, (3) engineers who helped rescue hundreds, (4) Army soldiers guard the San Antonio National Bank, (5) a soldier on Travis Street, as well as the Gunter Hotel on the right with floodwaters remaining, and (6) the survivors of the flood receiving food. The military continues to help San Antonio.

Famous Soldiers Once of San Antonio

This excerpt is from a booklet entitled *The Trail* from Camp Travis, dated October 28, 1921. From left to right are Gen. Ulysses S. Grant, Gen. Robert E. Lee, Theodore Roosevelt, Gen. Frederick Funston, Gen. James B. Harbord, and Gen. John Pershing.

This collection of images shows (1) a pilot putting the giant hawk to roost for the night, (2) pilots mowing the lawn, (3) some enlisted men fliers, (4) soldiers conducting an atmospheric test for the day, (5) the drawbacks of flying, (6) a plane in flight, (7) a football squad made up of good fellows and good pilots, and (9) General Pershing taking notice at Kelly Field.

Kelly Field was a great flying field that at one time contained approximately 2,000 acres. Kelly Field attained an international reputation for operations training. Picture no. 7 shows an ambulance and fire wagon.

This 1913 photograph taken at Fort Sam Houston shows a soldier digging through boxes, looking for mail or packages from home. The headquarters and garrison have always constituted one of the Army's most important commands. Note the small tents that housed the men.

A dress parade takes place at Fort Sam Houston in 1912. By this time, the military units at the fort included an infantry regiment and a regiment of cavalry, each with a headquarters and band; two batteries of field artillery; and signal and engineer troops. Throughout its existence, a close and harmonious relationship has prevailed between Fort Sam Houston and the city of San Antonio. The two have grown and matured together. The city often has been called the "mother-in-law of the Army" because so many soldiers, including Dwight D. Eisenhower, met their future spouses here.

The first airplane arrived in San Antonio in 1910 at Fort Sam Houston. This photograph shows two soldiers, from Fort Sam Houston, posed in studio prop depicting them flying in a biplane over Alamo Plaza. The nation's first flying school was located on Kelly Field. This same year, San Antonio experienced its first aviation death when Lt. George E.M. Kelly died.

In the 1870s, the construction of Fort Sam Houston began under the supervision of the military commander of the Department of Texas. By 1876, upon completion of the Quadrangle, the Army began to move its facilities to the new site. In 1886, the Quadrangle housed Geronimo and those Apaches captured with him while the federal government decided whether they were prisoners of war or common criminals.

The picture, published in the *Broadcaster*, a monthly paper for the employees of the public service company, shows a view of Randolph Air Force Base. Cadets where trained to be full-fledged pilots and officers of the Air Corps. Nearly 1,300 cadets started training every five weeks.

Pictured at left, the Masonic Building was used as the Bexar County Courthouse around 1872. It was located on the east side of Soledad Street. A view of the Veramendi Palace, named after merchant and public figure Fernando Veramendi, shows cowboys posing in the street. The Casino Building was used for the first social club in San Antonio, organized in 1854.

This is Commerce Street looking west toward city hall. It was designed by O. Kramer, constructed with local limestone, and completed in 1891. The cash and grocery store was beside a store that advertises bay oysters.

Robert E. Lee was stationed in San Antonio as the commander of the newly formed 2nd Cavalry Regiment of Texas in 1856. His headquarters was in the Vance House at the northeast corner of Houston and St. Mary's Streets. It was not until 1876 that a permanent Army base was authorized and construction began in San Antonio, Texas. In 1890, this permanent base was named Fort Sam Houston.

Coming down North Alamo Street, this military parade was held on Armistice Day. Veterans Day is a successor to Armistice Day, commemorating November 11, 1918, when the armistice was signed to end the fighting in World War I.

Dated June 24, 1909, the back of this postcard reads, "Teddy was here. Now Bill is coming too on Oct 19th to S.A." Bill refers to the name "Billy Possum," created by the Taft campaign to challenge "Teddy Bear." President Taft came to San Antonio on Oct 17, 1909, to help dedicate a new chapel at Fort Sam Houston.

Lila Cockrell received a bachelor of arts degree from Southern Methodist University (SMU) in Dallas and served in the US Navy as an ensign during World War II. Her public service includes serving as a San Antonio city councilwoman from 1963 to 1970 and again from 1973 to 1975. In 1975, she was elected mayor of San Antonio, becoming the first female to hold that position in any major Texas city, and she served until 1981 and again from 1989 to 1991. Mrs. Cockrell has served on a number of local, state, and national boards She currently holds the position of president of the San Antonio Parks Foundation. (Courtesy of the San Antonio Express-News.)

Pres. John F. Kennedy came to San Antonio a second time on November 21, 1963. After driving from the airport down Broadway Street, taking a left on Houston Street, and then onto Alamo Plaza, he gave a 30-minute speech. After leaving the Alamo, the motorcade drove down St. Mary's Street with the Granada, formerly the Plaza Hotel, in the background. Gov. John Connally and First Lady Jacqueline Kennedy are seen waving.

After spending just a little over two hours in San Antonio, the president and first lady boarded the presidential plane at Kelly Air Force Base for a flight to Houston, Texas. Below, they wave goodbye to the crowd at Kelly Air Force Base. (Courtesy of Mary Louise Peché.)

This military parade going east on Houston Street is the 2nd Platoon, 82nd Airborne Division. The S.H. Kress & Co. building on the right was originally constructed in 1939 and designed by architect Edward F. Sibbert in an Art Deco style.

Gen. Douglas MacArthur attended the West Texas Military Academy, now TMI–The Episcopal School of Texas, in San Antonio while his Father was stationed at Fort Sam Houston. He graduated as valedictorian and went on to West Point. He had an illustrious military career until Pres. Harry S. Truman removed him from his command on April 11, 1951. He came to San Antonio on a grassroots campaign to convince the American people his Korean War program was a better gamble for peace than President Truman's.

Four

BUILDINGS AND COMMERCE

Frost Bank's traditional company values
are the philosophical legacy of its founder-
patriarch, Col. Thomas Claiborne (T.C.)
Frost. Rarely in the history of American
industry has one man exerted so potent an
influence on an enterprise so many years
after its founding. He was the rarest of men,
a scholar blessed with an innate love of
books but also with an uncanny business
acumen and common horse sense. (Courtesy
of "Banking on Tradition" by Tom Walker)

This photograph of the Maverick Bank building at the corner of Alamo and Houston Streets was taken in 1907. The small canopy towers to the right are on the Moore building, constructed in 1904.

Looking south down Alamo Street on January 15, 1907, the photograph shows the Gallagher Building, the Paul Mueller Cutlery store with a banner, and the Joske Bros. store.

The Market House, designed by Alfred Giles, started in September 1899. The city razed the market in 1925 for street widening and a flood bypass channel. It took a year to complete and cost an estimated $55,000.

This Commerce Street photograph was taken looking west around 1925. St. Joseph's Catholic Church is on the right. Eventually, Joske's department store, whose premises later became part of Rivercenter Mall, would encompass the church on both sides. It was then referred to as St. Joske's. Fawcett Furniture later relocated to Dolorosa Street. (Courtesy of the Van Steenberg family.)

The Missouri-Kansas-Texas depot was built in 1917, and the towers were copied from Mission Concepcion. Before it was razed in 1968, it was located at South Flores Street and Durango Boulevard.

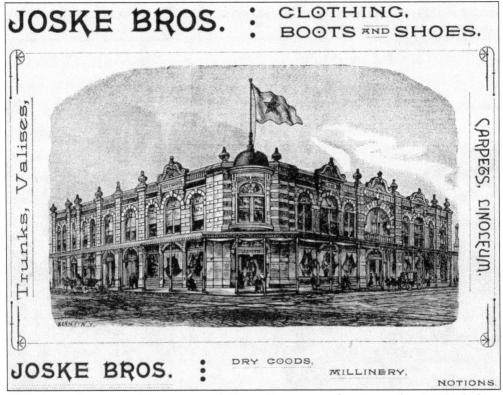

This store at the corner of Commerce and Alamo Streets opened on September 4, 1888. In June 1942, Joske Bros. installed the first escalators in San Antonio. On January 3, 1961, the store celebrated its 88th birthday by selling 45-rpm records at 5 for 98¢, and Bozo the Clown made an appearance for the kids.

This 1896 photograph was taken of Commerce Street looking west towards the Commerce Street Bridge. Bull Brothers Saloon can be seen just over the bridge on the left. This would later become Casa Rio. The Clifford Building, directly across the street, would house the office of Robert H.H. Hugman, architect of the River Walk. (Courtesy of the Van Steenberg family.)

This is a view of the San Antonio National Bank. At the time of this photograph, there were no less than four national banks and six private banks. The bank rate of interest was from 8 to 12 percent.

This photograph, taken from Alamo Plaza, shows the first Ford dealership in San Antonio just behind the walls of the Alamo. The Ford Motor Company sold the dealership to Clifton George in 1909. Frank M. Gillespie acquired the dealership in the 1930s, in part to help George settle his debts incurred by the construction of the Medical Arts Building, now know as the Emily Morgan Hotel. (Courtesy of the Van Steenberg family.)

This picture from 1907 shows the S.H. Kress & Co. store. Samuel H. Kress, born in Pennsylvania in July 1863, lived to the age of 92. The San Antonio store, located on Houston Street, was situated right next to the Bexar Hotel, and a new Kress store was built in 1938. The chain's stores began closing in the 1980s nationwide. San Antonio's Kress building is under renovation.

Samuel Maverick, born in 1803, moved to Texas, where there was available land, after his education. He was involved in the Texas Revolution of 1835 and left before the Battle of the Alamo in 1836. Samuel Maverick was one of the signers of the Texas Declaration of Independence. On May 5, 1884, construction of the Maverick Bank building began. Located at the corner of Alamo and Houston Streets, the structure was the tallest in San Antonio at the time. It had eight fireproof vaults and a water-powered elevator.

This photograph of the west side of Alamo Plaza shows the Reuter Building. It was originally designed by architect James Wahrenberger for William Reuter in 1891. Billy Reuter operated a very elegant saloon and ladies' parlor. When the Victorian bandstand was moved from Alamo Plaza to San Pedro Park in 1897, he built a replacement so his patrons would have a place to dance. (Courtesy of the Van Steenberg family.)

Opened on January 4, 1909, the St. Anthony Hotel is the third oldest hotel in San Antonio still in operation. It opened its roof garden in June 1915. In 1936, it was one the first hotels to get central air-conditioning.

Jose Cassiano was born in San Remo, Italy. In the 1820s, he moved to San Antonio, where he opened a store and acquired extensive property. During the Siege of Bexar, he turned his home and store over to the army. He served as a scout, and just before the attack on the Alamo, he sent messages to William B. Travis on the movements of Mexican general Antonio Lopez de Santa Anna. He contributed generously to San Fernando Cathedral. (Courtesy of the Van Steenberg family.)

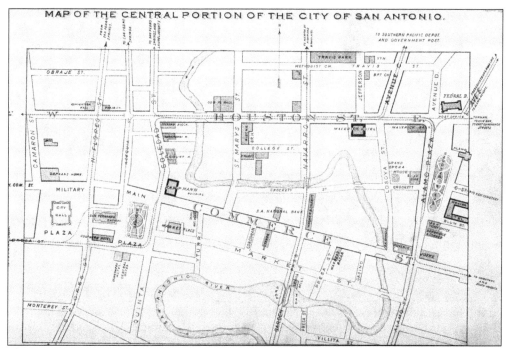

This map is from the book *San Antonio De Bexar* by William Corner, released for Christmas in 1890. In the preface, Corner writes, "I trust my book will not only be a satisfaction to the inquiring visitor, but I would like to think that it could furnish a few notes and suggestions to a future historian of Texas."

This is a photograph of the east side of Main Plaza. The storefronts are on Soledad Street, which intersects with Commerce Street to the left. After the Mexican War, peace and economic connections to the United States restored prosperity to the city, and by 1860, at the start of the Civil War, San Antonio had grown to a city of 15,000 people. This period saw a large emigration from Germany. There were many German merchants, and one was as likely to hear German as English or Spanish spoken on the streets of the city. (Courtesy of the Van Steenberg family.)

In this image, a streetcar passes by the Gunter Hotel on the left, the Majestic Theater is on the right, and at the very end of Houston Street, one can see the Medical Arts Building, now the Emily Morgan Hotel. The last streetcar ran on April 29, 1933, when 55 years of service came to an inglorious end as the tracks were ripped up and the remaining cars were either sold to other cities or for scrap.

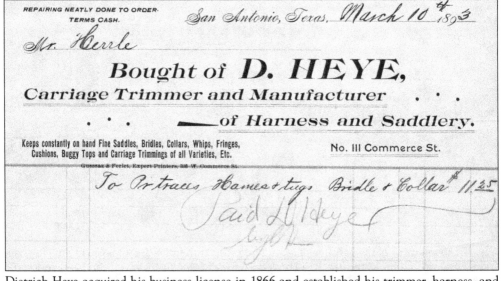

Dietrich Heye acquired his business license in 1866 and established his trimmer, harness, and saddle store in 1867. The store, still standing on Commerce Street, was family owned through four generations when it closed in the 1970s. At the time of closing, it was one of the oldest saddle companies in Texas.

The Frost Bros. department store originated in downtown San Antonio. It carried high-fashion pieces and employing personal shoppers when the first shop opened in 1917. The store was ranked with Neiman Marcus and Saks Fifth Avenue, even having its own in-house Gucci boutique at one point, and many still recall the grayish lavender dress boxes with a long-stemmed flower across the store's italicized logo. The store flourished until mid-1989, when it closed its doors. (Courtesy of the Van Steenberg family.)

First named Little's Shoe Hospital, this store was located on Commerce Street where the 22-floor Frost Bank building is now located. Second from left is Ben Little, and the man to the far right is Lucien Little. Established in 1915, the company, now known as Dave Little's Boots, has been owned and operated by the same family for almost 100 years. (Courtesy of Dave Little's Boots.)

Schilo's Delicatessen is a San Antonio institution. The authentic German deli, located in the heart of downtown San Antonio, has been serving authentic German cuisine since 1917. Schilo's is one of the oldest continually operated restaurants in the state of Texas. Housed in an old mercantile exchange building dating back to the 1800s, Schilo's embodies that time in San Antonio when the majority of the citizens were of German decent. The exchange's vault is now the walk-in refrigerator. Old signage, postcards, and tile flooring continue the German theme throughout the deli. (Courtesy of Raul Medina III.)

In 1941, Pete and Cruz Cortez opened a little three-table café for early-rising farmers and workers at San Antonio's El Mercado/Market Square. Sixty years later, Mi Tierra Café is a world-famous landmark. This is the place hometown regulars and hungry tourists go for authentic Mexican food and a warm Texas welcome.

This view of St. Mary's is dated from the 1880s. It is not known whether it was St. Mary's Institute (1853–1882) or St. Mary's College (1882–1893) at the time this image was captured. The architect who designed the old Ursuline Academy, Francois Giraud, also designed this school. In this photograph, two boys hold baseball bats. (Courtesy of the Marianist Archives, San Antonio.)

There are two Brass Era Model Ts in the background on this image. The delivery truck displays the company name on the side: Alamo. The most interesting vehicle is towards the left of the picture, which might be a hot food truck as it's too early to be a passenger bus and the configuration of the windows suggests something is being served through them; also, it features rolled-up canvas covers. This corner site at St. Mary's and College Streets is now the Charline McCombs Empire Theatre. This pictured could have been taken at the start of construction on November 9, 1913, when two Houston Street landmarks—the Iron Front Saloon and the Empire Theater—were torn down and replaced with a modern building, according to Hugh Hemphill. (Courtesy of the Marianist Archives, San Antonio.)

On March 19, 1912, Edward Rand bought the Garza homestead for $200,000. This city block would become the Wolff & Marx Company in 1913. Albert Wolff and Daniel Marx had the tallest building at that time. The department store closed in 1965, when it was sold to the rival Joske Bros. It was eventually saved from demolition by the San Antonio Conservation Society, sold again in 1968, and is now called the Rand Building.

This view faces west toward Houston Street from Jefferson Street. On the right are the Kress store, the St. James Hotel, and the L.P. Peck furniture store.

Five

FESTIVALS AND ENTERTAINMENT

One of the first known pins, this was produced nine years after the first Battles of the Flowers Parade. Collecting Fiesta San Antonio pins and medals is said to go back some 50 years, according to the organization. This colorful pin suggests that this six-day celebration was called the San Antonio Street Fair. It was made by Whitehead & Hoag Co. of Newark, New Jersey.

The Parade of Nations came up Alamo Street on Wednesday, April 20, 1927. The floats decorated to represent 15 different nationalities in San Antonio were: Sweden with a Viking motif; Ireland with a massive castle; China with its dragons; Germany with the Lorelei motif; Mexico with Mayan-style architecture; Austria with a castle scene; Italy with a scenic fountain and Maria Lucchese as queen; Greece, representing the Parthenon with Nick Morosis in charge for the new Greek church; Switzerland, represented by the Alps and a cottage, with G. Zeilleger in charge; France with a Joan of Arc motif; Japan with a delightful tea garden float; Holland with a windmill and flowers float; Canada with the Northwest Mounted Police and a princess; Britain, represented by the British lions and governed by the Queen with Texas-British society president Florence Gross; and the United States (pictured), with the goddess Liberty, Uncle Sam, and a soldier, sailor, and marine under the auspices of the Eighth Corps Area, US Army, Lt. Col. Charles F. Martin in charge.

This photograph was provided by Jean Bloomingdale, whose dad, Eugene Ford, and a Mr. Stevens decorated this car for the Battle of Flowers Parade. Fiesta San Antonio, previously called Fiesta San Jacinto, is a 10-day festival held every spring in San Antonio. It originated in 1891 as a salute to the heroes of the Battles of the Alamo and San Jacinto.

Both these are real-photo postcards showing views of the float representing Mexico in the Parade of Nations on April 20, 1927. The parade is going north on Alamo Street. To the right is Woolworth's five and dime department store.

The San Antonio Conservation Society (the sponsor of this parade entry) was founded in 1924. It is one of the oldest and most active community preservation groups in the United States. The society has been responsible for saving most of the historical attractions that make San Antonio one of the top destinations in Texas. The Battle of Flowers Parade is the only one in the country to be planned and directed completely by women. Today, it's the largest parade in Fiesta. It's second in size nationally only to the Tournament of Roses Parade.

The Jefferson Lasso drill team marches west on Commerce Street during the Battle of Flowers Parade. The group, founded by Constance "Connie" Douglas in 1932, made the cover of *Life* magazine in 1938. In its heyday, it had more 150 girls.

This group of cowboys 50 strong rides east on Commerce Street. To the right is city hall with a Sky Ride in front. The buildings along the street are a liquor store, the Bargain Store, and the Max Sheff store, which specializes in clothing, shoes, and "Ladies' Ready-to-Wear."

By 1895, the Fiesta celebration had developed into a weeklong event. The first queen, chosen in 1896, was Ida Archer of Austin, and a king was chosen in 1897. In 1901, the parade included its first horseless vehicle. By 1916, the parade had grown so much in scope that the floats could no longer be decorated with fresh flowers, so artificial flowers were used instead.

In 1937, the San Antonio Conservation Society planned a one-day Native American Festival along the banks of the San Antonio River to celebrate the heritage of the city's early settlers while raising funds for historic preservation. This became one of Fiesta's more popular celebrations and gave rise to the event's expansion and official naming as A Night In Old San Antonio (NIOSA) in 1948. What began with a handful of society ladies has grown into a huge undertaking staffed by over 16,000 volunteers who setup and man the annual four-night event each April. The historic downtown village of La Villita is its venue as 85,000 visitors now come through the gates during NIOSA.

May 5, celebrated as Cinco de Mayo, commemorates the Mexican army's 1862 victory over France at the Battle of Puebla during the Franco-Mexican War (1861–1867). A relatively minor holiday in Mexico, in the United States, Cinco de Mayo has evolved into a celebration of Mexican culture and heritage, particularly in areas with large Mexican-American populations such as San Antonio. The celebrations include parades, mariachi music performances, street festivals, and young women dancing in colorful dresses.

This picture shows the entrance to Mission Stadium during a Jehovah's Witness convention in July 1954.

This sign was erected on the proposed site of a baseball park. Spirited civic-minded leader and funeral director Peter Loring loved the sport of baseball. Mission Stadium opened in 1937 and closed in 1964.

Controversy surrounded the filming of *Viva Max* due to its content (it was a parody of the Battle of the Alamo), and certain historical groups objected to the filming of the Alamo. The movie stopped production, and some scenes were filmed at an Alamo replica in Brackettville, Texas. Remaining scenes with Pamela Tiffin had to be shot in Italy where she was working. (Courtesy of Ernestine Seik.)

Keenan Wynn, as General Lacomber in *Viva Max,* signs an autograph on the back of local Eino Seik. Peter Ustinov, as Gen. Maximilian Rodriguez De Santos, stands to the side. (Courtesy of Ernestine Seik.)

Harry Morgan (right), before his stardom from the television series *Dragnet* and M*A*S*H, poses with a fan. Morgan played chief of police Sylvester in the movie *Viva Max*. (Courtesy of Ernestine Seik.)

Jonathan Winters, who played Gen. Billy Joe Hallson, signs autographs. (Courtesy of Ernestine Seik.)

John Astin, who played Sergeant Valdez, looks at the camera. He was 38 at the time *Viva Max* was released. Pamela Tiffin takes a break talks with another actor in front of the Alamo doors. (Courtesy of Ernestine Seik.)

Gary Cooper, looking at the camera, had a small part in the first movie to be filmed in San Antonio: *Wings*. This movie won the first Academy Award for Best Picture. Gary Cooper stands next to Sgt. Eugene Ford at Stinson Field.

October 28, 1982, officially became "Carlos Santana Day" in San Antonio. Mayor Henry Cisneros presented Carlos Santana the proclamation for his part in helping raise monies for the city-wide fundraiser *Telethon Navideno*. Also included in this effort were KTFM Radio and Stone City Attractions. Santana was in town for a Stone City Attractions concert at the San Antonio Convention Center Arena. Pictured from left to right are Mayor Henry Cisneros, Carlos Santana and president and executive producer of Stone City Attractions Jack Orbin. (Courtesy of Stone City Attractions.)

The MVP award always calls a window seat; Tim Duncan, the MVP of the 1999 championship team, would want it this way. The first San Antonio Spurs NBA Championship trophy claimed the aisle seat. It would be a trip both trophies would make again, when San Antonio later swept Cleveland in four games in 2007.

On Saturday June 26, 1999, Steve Kerr, five-time NBA champion (left), Avery Johnson, holding San Antonio's first NBA Championship Trophy, David Robinson, and the team mascot, the Coyote, exit the plane to a reported 10,000-plus awaiting fans. Author David L. Peché and his brother Albert Peché attended this joyous moment in San Antonio history.

This photograph was taken on June 18, 1999, the second game against the New York Knicks in the NBA Finals. There was 16 Silver Dancer cheerleaders on the team, and Stephanie Reyes (pictured) entertained the fans from 1997 to 2002. When the Spurs won the NBA title in 1999, the Silver Dancers where also a part of the first River Parade celebration. Stephanie remembers the intensity at the Alamodome and the excitement of the team's first championship.

Every Good Friday since 1986, thousands have gathered to watch a dramatic reenactment of the crucifixion in front of San Fernando Cathedral. The passion play is one of the most elaborate in the world and draws as many as 25,000 people downtown. It begins its procession with Christ bearing his cross at Milan Park. The cathedral's parishioners take on the roles of Pontius Pilate, Roman soldiers, and Jesus Christ himself.

Luminaria is San Antonio's annual celebration of art and artists. Held in March and overseen by San Antonio's creative leaders, it is free of charge and showcases all art forms in an outdoor setting and inside various venues downtown. Luminaria spotlights San Antonio's cultural assets for local citizens and visitors alike and is made possible through the generosity of artists, arts organizations, volunteers, and public and private donations. Held at HemisFair Park, an estimated 300,000 people attended Luminaria in 2012.

Avery Johnson's last shot won game five in New York to give the city its first NBA trophy in 1999. Johnson is holding the trophy; the man to the right of him in sunglasses is David Robinson, who was 33 at the time; he stayed on to help the Spurs win another title. Robinson continues to live in San Antonio, established Carver Academy, and was inducted in the Naismith Memorial Basketball Hall of Fame.

MVP Tim Duncan raises his arms in celebration of his first championship. The 23-year-old, 6-foot-11 athlete eventually added three more championship rings.

The Fiesta Flambeau Parade is the largest illuminated night parade in the nation. It travels along the 2.6-mile parade route through downtown San Antonio. It is estimated that there are 600,000 spectators along the streets of San Antonio and another 1.5 million in the television viewing audience. The University of Texas Longhorn Band is the premier band that traditionally leads the parade each year.

The Texas Folklife Festival was modeled after the Smithsonian's Folklife Festival. On behalf of the Institute of Texan Cultures (which was built as part of the Texan Pavilion for the 1968 World's Fair), O.T. Baker attended the first Smithsonian Folklife Festival and returned home with big plans to duplicate the event in San Antonio. One is able to experience the delicious cuisine, traditional dances, fine-crafted keepsakes, storytelling, and music of more than 40 ethnic groups at the biggest three-day cultural celebration in Texas. Under the direction of Jo Ann Andera, the event celebrated its 42nd year in 2012. This photograph shows two participants enjoying themselves on the seesaw.

Rosita Fernandez, a longtime San Antonian and pioneer of Tejano music, gained international fame as a recording artist and movie star. She was a humanitarian and ambassador for San Antonio as well as a mother and wife. She was known as "San Antonio's First Lady of Song," a title that was given to her in 1968 by Lady Bird Johnson. This photograph was taken at Luminaria; the portrait was painted by renowned San Antonio artist Jesse Trevino.

Selena Quintanilla Perez (April 16, 1971–March 31, 1995), known by many simply as Selena, was a Mexican-American singer-songwriter and "Queen of Tejano Music" and was seen as an icon by many. After an argument about some missing monies from her boutiques, she fired Yolanda Saldivar, the manager of her two shops. Selena met with her to recover some financial documents in a Corpus Christi hotel. Saldivar shot Selena in the back as she was leaving, killing her almost instantly. Although born in Lake Jackson, Selena was adopted by San Antonio.

Six

RIVER WALK AND FLOODS

The lead visionary and original architect on the River Walk project was Robert H.H. Hugman. He was appointed to the project and work began in 1939. Although not as extensive as his original proposal, the WPA project resulted in the improvement of more than 21 blocks along the river, including the construction of 17,000 feet of walkways, 31 stairways leading from 21 bridges, and the planting of more than 11,000 trees and shrubs.

This picture of the flood of 1913 on St. Mary's Street looking south shows an "Auto Mermaid." A man stands on the roof of the Carter-Mullay Transfer Company building to the right. The Hertzberg clock is just barely seen further up the street in front of the Gunter Building.

The Army floats down St. Mary's Street on September 21, 1921. Across the street is San Antonio's fourth Piggly Wiggly store. Underneath the store name reads, "All over the World." The Victoria Hotel is just ahead, the Gunter Hotel on the right, and Hotel Lanier is off of Travis Street.

The flood of September 1921 had water downtown over six feet high in some areas. On Riegler's Confectionery store, the watermark can be seen. This building is occupied by the Palm Restaurant as of 2012. The building to the right, built in 1919, was the South Texas Building and is now the Home 2 Suites by Hilton. The flood was responsible for the death of approximately 51 people, and countless others went missing. The city's needed floodwater control was completed on December 11, 1926, when the Olmos Dam was dedicated.

The December flood of 1913 is documented in this image facing south down St. Mary's Street at Houston Street with a few kids smiling for the camera. The last 10 days of November 1913 saw heavy rains that laid the foundation for flooding during the first five days of December.

This view of the Eli Hertzberg clock shows civilians milling about in awe. The clock was moved here from Commerce Street in October 1910. The "Auto Mermaid" car is in the distance. (Courtesy of the Marianist Archives, San Antonio.)

This photograph by Ernst W. Raba shows College Street. Raba was an early San Antonio photographer who was born in Friedland, Bohemia. He came to San Antonio at the age of 17 to apprentice as a photographer. He had his own studio by the age of 26 and most notably photographed President Taft laying the cornerstone to the Post Chapel on October 22, 1909. (Courtesy of the Marianist Archives, San Antonio.)

San Antonio helped celebrate the Spurs' championship with a river parade, the first of its kind. One person holds up a sign that reads "End of a Journey." An estimated quarter-million fans came down to the River Walk to celebrate.

Construction of Central Catholic High School took place along the San Antonio River in 1931–1932. The river would be redirected a few years later. Seen is St. Mary's Street. (Courtesy of the Marianist Archives, San Antonio.)

This photograph was taken with the Commerce Street Bridge in the background. This was the first bridge to span the River Walk. Casa Rio restaurant is to the left. The city's most popular attraction, it is often crowded and filled with children, partygoers, tourists, and locals. In the heart of the River Walk is an area filled with restaurants, shops, and nightclubs, punctuated by fountains and towering cypress trees. Paddleboats were fun for residents and tourists alike, but they were finally dry-docked when they became too dangerous.

The Texas Cavaliers River Parade is one of the premier events each year during San Antonio's biggest celebration, Fiesta. Approximately 250,000 spectators are treated to the sights and sounds of a parade that winds its way through the heart of downtown on the San Antonio River. Pictured on the barge is the US Army Old Fife and Drum Corps. It has participated in Fiesta events since the early 1980s.

At 7:00 p.m. on the Friday following Thanksgiving, the switch is thrown and approximately 1,500,000 twinkling lights form a magical canopy over San Antonio's River Walk. The lights shine brightly every evening through January 1. The lighting ceremony is the official kickoff to the Paseo Del Rio Holiday Festival. The spectacular one-hour parade along San Antonio's River Walk features decorated, illuminated floats with celebrities, bands, and lavishly costumed participants.

Joyous caroling fills the evening air along the San Antonio River Walk as more than 185 school, church, company, and civic choral groups ring in the holidays by singing traditional carols on cruising boats. The nightly caroling and sing-along winds its way along the river until 9:45 p.m. Pictured are some members of the Downtown Residents Association enjoying their night on the river.

Founded in 1946 by Alfred F. Beyer, the Casa Rio restaurant was the first San Antonio business to open its doors to the river and take advantage of the waterway's setting. Canoes, gondolas, and paddleboats, evolving into tour and dinner boats, began here and helped create the River Walk of today. (Courtesy of Casa Rio.)

This image, captured a few years later, shows the addition of a canopy over the front door. Casa Rio once listed its address as 100 W. Commerce Street. For a short time, it also opened Casa Rio Bar-B-Q Restaurant on the River and was located at 231 South Broadway Street, one block from Joske Bros.

This picture, taken looking north on the river before the east side had a walkway, shows the Houston Street Bridge.

This view exhibits an era when paddleboats were used on the river. The giant cypress tree pictured is said to have been used by a Mexican sniper to shoot Benjamin R. Milam on the night of December 7, 1835.

This real-photo postcard's image was taken from the Navarro Street Bridge looking west. The St. Mary's Bridge is ahead. A covered gondola from Casa Rio and canoes enjoy the river. The waterfall is still there next to the Omni La Mansion del Rio, a four-diamond hotel.

This theater was named after Edwin Arneson and constructed in 1939. During the summer of 1965, the Arneson River Theater ran a summer river festival that featured a boat ride down the San Antonio River for an evening of entertainment including music, dances, and songs of Old Mexico. Rosita's Bridge, named for Rosita Fernandez, is in the background.

Seven

HemisFair Park
and La Villita

On December 22, 1966, the city council approved a contract for the construction of a 622-foot-tall tower for HemisFair 1968 and sold $5.5 million in bonds to pay for the structure. On January 23, 1968, the top of the Tower of the Americas was put into place.

This picture, taken on March 30, 1968, captures a rush of activity, as some of the exhibits for the World's Fair were not ready. The fair opened on April 6, 1968, two days after Martin Luther King Jr. was assassinated.

Fiesta Island, south of the Tower of the Americas, was the heart of the rides and games area of HemisFair. It features 18 major rides, surrounded by snack stands, souvenir stalls, and games of skill and chance. The area is landscaped with walks and waterways, shaded sitting areas, and tree-lined paths. (Courtesy of *HemisFair Guidebook,* 1968.)

The Sky Ride went from Las Plazas del Mundo to the Institute of Texan Cultures, and the cost for a ride was 50¢. Eleven Sky Rides in the air was a sight to see at the 1968 World's Fair.

Mariachi goes beyond music, it is the sum of a cultural revolution expressed through a group of musicians, dressed in popular clothing (most recently charro suits) which encompasses the essence of Mexico and its people. It is something cultural, spiritual and traditional that is unique to its country, an experience not to be missed. The word *mariachi* refers to the musicians now commonly seen in restaurants or strolling the streets, dressed in silver-studded charro outfits with wide-brimmed hats playing a variety of instruments including violins, guitars, basses, *vihuelas* (a 5-string guitar) and trumpets. Their songs speak about machismo, love, betrayal, death, politics, revolutionary heroes, and even animals (one particularly famous song is "La Cucaracha"). Mariachi originated in the southern part of the state of Jalisco some time in the 19th century.

Pictured here are puppets from the *Les Poupées de Paris* variety show, created by puppeteer Sid Krofft and his brother Marty Krofft. The Krofft brothers presented an original show called *Kaleidoscope*. They performed two different shows: one for children and a risqué version for adults.

The *Danza de los Voladores de Papantla* (Dance of Papantla's Flyers) is an ancient, dramatic ritual dance from Veracruz, Mexico. Five men, representing the five elements of the indigenous world, climb to the top of a pole; one of them stays, playing a flute and dancing, while four others descend the 114-foot pole with a rope tied to one of their feet. The rope unwraps itself 13 times for each of the four flyers, representing the 52 weeks of the year.

Los Voladores de Papantla performed ancient dramatic rituals. The 400-year-old ceremony represented the Indians' descent from the heavens. The flyers represent birds and the tribe's belief that when one dies, he returns to earth as a bird. Pictured here, the men perform at the Pepsi–Frito Lay Pavilion.

The chief's daughter prepares for supreme sacrifice. Human sacrifice has been practiced on a number of different occasions and in many different cultures. The various rationales behind human sacrifice are the same that motivate religious sacrifice in general. Human sacrifice is intended to bring good fortune and to pacify the gods.

IBM–Durango Pavilion was where one could watch a computer instruct a loom to weave patterns on fabric. Using a light pen, visitors could doodle a design on the computer's television-like screen. When the computer received the design, it directed the loom to recreate the identical pattern on a small square of fabric.

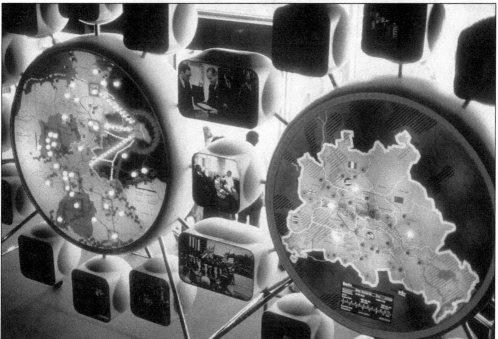

According to the HemisFair guidebook, the Germany Pavilion "effectively demonstrates a tangible reciprocity between the old world and the new. In particular, the exhibit provides a survey of German contributions to the development of Texas and the southwest. The pavilion takes a look at life within the Federal republic of Germany and its key city, Berlin."

The Pearl Pavilion housed the 19th-century Palm Garden restaurant. The main building featured an exhibit, dining, and a bar and entertainment space for period-style performances. The smaller building was a retail shop for Judson Candies, a Pearl subsidiary.

Fairgoers had a variety of restaurants and eateries to choose from. They were spread out across the fairgrounds. Food areas provided fine cuisine from around the world as well as traditional fair favorites. Some of the old homes that were not demolished served as restaurants for some of the participating nations.

The mini-monorail consisted of an elevated track creating a 1.5-mile-long loop around the site and featuring three stations. Built by Universal Design, Ltd., each train consisted of a motorcar at each end and several passenger cars. One neat design feature was that the track ran through the IBM Lakeside Pavilion. The three passenger stations were near the Texas Pavilion, the General Electric Pavilion, and the foreign nations section.

The water-ski show took place in the three-acre lake at Fiesta Island and was sponsored by Mercury Outboard. Professional water skiers jumped off of ski ramps. The show was performed on a small artificial lake and featured several performances through the day. The outer section of the lake was used for the lagoon cruise, while the performing space was confined to the inner section.

The canal boat was a unique way to get around the grounds. Visitors enjoyed the view from the waterways, which offered them a vision of the fairgrounds from a different perspective. It was also a cooler way to travel, since the boats did not suffer from the radiant heat of the concrete walkways.

The Theater of the Performing Arts, fronted with a magnificent mural by Juan O'Gorman, featured a large variety of visiting performers and performances, including Vicki Carr and George Kirby, Bayanihan Philippine Dancers, Allen & Rossi and Joanie Sommers, Dixieland Jazz Festival, Jack Benny, Jimmy Dean, Wayne Newton, Bob Newhart, *Fiddler on the Roof*, Ravi Shankar, and the Houston Symphony with Andre Previn.

The Canadian Pavilion featured a multiscreen theater that showed visitors the history of Canada and its people. The HemisFair guidebook describes it as "Touched by subtle humor and the deft color of a distinctive folklore, the Canada Pavilion draws its visitor into a world that is both different and familiar. Multicultural in its origins and in its subsequent development, Canada today has just stepped into its second century of national life." (Courtesy of *HemisFair Guidebook*, 1968.)

The City of San Antonio marked its 250th birthday with HemisFair 1968, a six-month-long international exposition. Its theme was "Confluence of Civilizations in the Americas." Six and a half million people from around the world attended the celebration of the many ethnic groups that settled the western hemisphere. According to the souvenir book, "It presented visitors with a glittering panorama of national and corporate inventiveness; industrial progress, the far reaches of education, the splendor of the arts, the wit and skill of the craftsman, and the humor and gaiety of the people." (Courtesy of *Official Souvenir Book*.)

HemisFair Park consisted of 92.6 acres. Looking down and straight ahead was the area of Las Plazas del Mundo, where 22 countries participated. The long building on the right of the bridge was the Republic of Mexico pavilion. It was one of the largest national exhibits and offered visitors a quick introduction to ancient traditions.

This is an image of the US Pavilion taken from the Hilton Hotel. The pavilion, situated on a 4.59-acre site adjacent to the international area, echoed the fair's theme with "Confluence USA." It was a two-building complex featuring an exhibit structure and a massive circular theater. With additional construction, it was subsequently converted to serve as the federal courthouse.

Pictured here from left to right are Gov. John Connally of Texas; H.B. Zachry, HemisFair 1968 board chairman; Frank Manupelli, executive vice president of the fair, and Walter W. McAllister Sr., mayor of San Antonio. The group gathered to announce plans for the fair at a press conference at the New York Hilton Hotel.

This photograph was produced by the *Christian Science Monitor* and taken by R. Norman Matheny on July 13, 1975. The Tower of the Americas' name was suggested by Rosa Gonzalez of Corpus Christi and became the official name of the 622-foot-fall HemisFair tower. The runner-up names included Hemispire, Hemistower, Astroshaft, Astrospire, Astrotower, Stratospire, Spire of the Americas, and Tower of Peace.

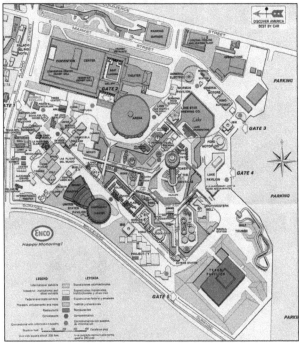

HemisFair was a fitting salute to the confluence of civilizations that is the western world, and it is only fitting that the six-month international exposition was a part of the 250th anniversary of San Antonio.

La Villita was San Antonio's first neighborhood. It was originally a settlement of primitive huts for the Spanish soldiers stationed at the Mission San Antonio Valero, or the Alamo. After a flood in 1819, brick, stone, and adobe houses replaced the earlier structures. In 1836, La Villita was the site of General Santa Anna's cannon line in the Battle of the Alamo, and a map from that year showed the village to be of considerable size.

The Bombach House was constructed in 1847. Otto Bombach, a carpenter, built the first two-story structure in San Antonio for his family. It was thereafter utilized as a boardinghouse, a grocery story and bar, a private school, and a hangout for desperados. The lower rooms of the building, once hidden under silt, were rediscovered during renovation in 1950.

The land bought by Samuel W. McAllister on which he built his house and store was incorporated into La Villita in 1949. McAllister migrated from Kentucky to San Antonio before the Civil War and served as justice of the peace as well as judge of the corporation court of Bexar County. The McAllister House & Store may have been built in two stages, as the first story is made of limestone and the second story is comprised of caliche block. Today, it is Guadalajara Grill and Mustang Grey's. (Courtesy of La Villita Historic Village.)

Rafael Herrera bought this piece of land in 1854 and built this house, later named the San Martin House. Don Jose de San Martin was the first president of Peru and fought for independence in Argentina, Chile, and Peru. The photograph also shows the 30-story Smith-Young Tower, the Plaza Hotel just behind it, and the A.B. Frank Company, a dry good and groceries wholesaler with a water tower on the roof.

Early in his administration, Mayor Maury Maverick began a project he was proud of: the restoration of the historic Spanish village La Villita ("the Little Town"), in the heart of San Antonio. On August 3, 1939, supported by a grant from the National Youth Administration, 25 youths began to clean up the area that was to become the now-famous tourist attraction and center of San Antonio's festive and cultural activities.

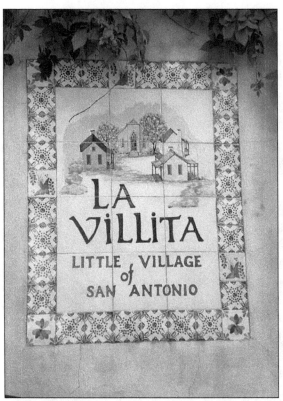

La Villita is a restoration, carried out in 1939 as a Works Progress Administration (WPA) program, of the Spanish-Mexican village that originally stood on the site. There are historic houses, artisans' shops, art galleries, restaurants, a river theater, and a nondenominational church. La Villita extends along Villita Street between Presa and Alamo Streets just south of the river, an easy stroll from most downtown hotels.

The Arneson River Theater is an open-air theater designed by Robert H.H. Hugman and erected in 1939 in La Villita on the San Antonio River. It was named after Edwin Arneson, who was instrumental in securing the funds to develop the River Walk. The audience sits on the grass-covered south side of the river, across from the stage.

Eight

THEN AND NOW

On March 31, 1968, the "world's most unusual hotel" was dedicated in San Antonio when the Hilton Palacio del Rio opened its doors in time for HemisFair. The 500-room, 22-story hotel built by H.B. Zachry was completed 10 months after architects started work on the plans. The facade was lit like the flag a few days after the 9/11 terrorist attack. (Courtesy of Raul Medina III.)

The vehicle in the foreground is a c. 1921 Ford Model T Runabout. The ride is being powered by a Fordson tractor of the same era. The front wheels do not have tires, which might have helped with belt traction, according to Hugh Hemphill. (Courtesy of the Marianist Archives, San Antonio.)

The Fiesta carnival has moved from downtown to the side of the Alamodome. Attractions included the 130-foot-tall Mega Drop and the Drag Strip Mega Slide. The Drag Strip, specially designed for Wade Shows carnival company, is the largest American portable slide. Of course, the Ferris wheel will always be a carnival classic.

The Fairmont Hotel was built in 1906. The hotel's structure is classic Victorian, and each of its 37 rooms is unique. The hotel's future was shaky in 1984 due to the construction of Rivercenter Mall. Luckily, a year later, it was moved by a crane five blocks from its original location to 401 South Alamo Street. Total restoration cost $4 million. Standing atop the moving rig is Dru Van Steenberg. (Courtesy of the Van Steenberg family.)

This is a photograph of Dru Van Steenberg taken on October 19, 2012, as she stands in front of the Fairmount Hotel holding a newspaper article about the historical move. Robert D. Tips, a San Antonio businessman, walked by the Fairmount one day and decided to buy it and restore it to its pride and beauty. That was in June 2004, and, as renovations approached completion at the end of 2006, the Fairmount looked magnificent.

Houston Street is pictured looking east, with the Gunter Hotel to the left and the Empire and Majestic Theaters on the right. The Majestic was the second largest theater in the country. Because of its size, it was not only utilized to show movies but also featured entertainers from the Vaudeville circuit. Legendary stars that performed at the Majestic include Jack Benny, Mickey Rooney, Ann Miller, George Burns, and Bob Hope. In 1913, Thomas Brady built the Empire Theatre on the same site that had housed many theaters before it. It was built as a European palazzo and designed by architects Mauran, Russell & Crow of St. Louis.

Pictured is author David L. Peché holding his newspaper advertisement from ZZ Top's November 26, 1975, visit to San Antonio. Tickets cost $5.00, $6.50 and $7.50 and were promoted by Alex Cooley and Stone City Attractions. ZZ Top played these two nights in 2012, their first return since 2007. (Courtesy of Raul Medina III.)

Families from the Canary Islands came to Main Plaza, also referred to as Plaza de Islas. This is where the 16 Canary Islanders made their permanent settlement. Their one-story homes encircled the area. Some of their descendants still live in San Antonio. After the Civil War, these homes were replaced by masonry commercial and government structures.

The renovation of Main Plaza was a pet project of Mayor Phillip Hardberger and Fr. David Garcia, rector of San Fernando Cathedral. The project was completed in 2008 to the tune of $12 million. To protect this gathering space from traffic, the two thoroughfares on the east and west sides of the plaza were closed. Interactive fountains were installed and tall canopy shades were erected due to the lack of shade. A nonprofit organization, Main Plaza Conservancy, manages the day-to-day operations.

The first boys' school in San Antonio is still one of the largest all-male private secondary schools in the state of Texas. Central Catholic High School remains a prestigious landmark in San Antonio and a symbol throughout South Texas of teaching excellence. The three-story building, designed by Henry Dreisoerner, was dedicated in January 1932 with 226 boys enrolled and a Marianist faculty of 17. (Courtesy of the Marianist Archives, San Antonio.)

Central Catholic High School, which first opened in two rooms over a livery stable near San Fernando Cathedral in 1852, moved several times before settling into its current campus in the early 1930s. In 2011, the school announced an addition at an estimated cost of $3 million as part of about $15.5 million in upgrades at the 12-acre campus. (Courtesy of Raul Medina III.)

This photograph, taken in September 1947 looking south on Navarro Street, is of the O.R. Mitchell Used Car building. It appears that the company shared this building with WOAI Radio at the time. This building later became WOAI Radio and TV. Even as late as the 1960 and 1970s, O.R. Mitchell's new car lot was located at 1100 Broadway Street at Jones Avenue.

Pictured are, from left to right, John Gerard, a certified broadcast meteorologist with over 30 years of television experience; Emmy Award–winning journalist Delaine Mathieu; Randy Beamer, recipient of four Emmy Awards and an Edward R. Murrow Award; Emmy-nominated Elsa Ramon, whose first job was as a kid reporter for a show called *Kids World* in Austin; and Don Harris, a two-time Emmy Award–winning weekday sports anchor and sports director with 23 years at WOAI. (Courtesy of Raul Medina III and David Peché.)

Owned by Sheraton Hotels, the Gunter today is still one of the most classic hotels in San Antonio. With new development bringing Houston Street back to its prime, one can agree that the Gunter is still "at the Center of Everything." (Courtesy of Raul Medina III.)

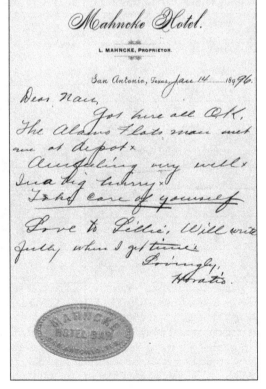

This letter and bar token are one of the few remaining pieces left of ephemera from the Ludwig Mahncke Hotel. Tokens were made to pay vendors, who would then use them at the establishment. The sender, Horatio, would write another letter from the Alamo Flats describing how bad the coffee and food were.

St. Mary Street is still one of the busiest streets in downtown; the Tower Life building dominates the skyline of this view. Sadly, the Blue Bonnet Hotel was razed in 1985. This view will change again in a few years when the addition of the VIA light-rail project. (Courtesy of Raul Medina III.)

On November 11, 1930, radio station KMAC, the city's newest radio broadcasting unit, with studios in the Blue Bonnet Hotel, made its formal debut with Mayor C.M. Chambers and other prominent civic and business leaders present to open the airwaves. Its call letters were KMAC in honor of its owner, William W. MacAllister.

Over recent years, Brackenridge Park has lost many of its most popular attractions. Sadly, the Sky Ride was removed from the park in 2001 because of contract issues and safety concerns. The city has done a good job of adding new hike and bike trails and giving the park a natural face-lift. The *Eagle* still runs proud through the park, and Brackenridge is still a great place for San Antonians to spend a day and have a picnic. (Courtesy of Raul Medina III.)

The Brackenridge Park *Eagle* and Sky Ride are pictured. In the good old days, a day at the zoo included a ride on the train and the Sky Ride. The *Eagle* is one of the longest miniature train rides in the United States at 3.2 miles, taking riders to different points of interest through the park. The Sky Ride, built in 1964 at a cost of $300,000, was proposed to the city by Red McCombs and Austin Hemphill. Colorful zoo animal–painted gondolas gave riders a panoramic view of the park and downtown San Antonio. (Courtesy of Raul Medina III.)

Located in the midst of historic downtown San Antonio, the Majestic Theater has long been regarded as one of the most ornate theaters in the United States. The theater was built in 1929 with 2,311 seats, making it the largest theater in Texas and the second largest motion picture theater in the nation. La Casas Foundation restored the building in 1989, and it was listed as a National Historic Landmark in 1993. (Courtesy of the Van Steenberg family.)

The Majestic Theater is pictured as it looks today. Joci Strauss founded Las Casas foundation. Using her unique ability to raise dollars from both individuals and corporations, she wooed potential donors with lunches on the Majestic stage. She possessed a passion for the historical buildings at the heart of downtown. Mrs. Strauss raised $5 million in 11 months, earning the gratitude of all of San Antonio. Eventually, Las Casas would raise three quarters of the total restoration cost of $15.5 million.

When the Spanish arrived for good in 1718, they immediately began constructing a system of irrigation ditches, or *acequias*, to divert water from the San Antonio River and San Pedro Creek to farmlands. At first, the work was carried out by the missionaries themselves and settlers, but most building was eventually carried out using forced labor of Indian converts. The acequias served as San Antonio's water system for almost 200 years and were the first municipal water distribution system in North America. They were remarkable engineering feats for their time, and some are still in use. This photograph was published by M.E Jacobson, 2 East Houston Street.

One hundred years later, the expansion and beautiful river are pictured. So much has been done to take care and enhance the River Walk. (Courtesy of Raul Medina III.)

This photograph of the 2nd Division Army Band was taken in front of the Alamo in 1920. Many millions of photographs have been taken with the Alamo in the background. Many ceremonies have been held in front of the Alamo. To say this is the most renowned building in Texas and possibly the entire United States would be putting it mildly.

The ladies posing for photographs in front of the Alamo in 2001 are members of Flushing Hospital School of Nursing, class of 1959. For most of them, it was their first trip to this fair city, and they couldn't be more impressed. This book's coauthor hosted the reunion.

The Joe and Harry Freeman Coliseum, built in 1949, has held numerous events for San Antonio. The 10,000-seat coliseum has been the site for the Stock Show and Rodeo. The land that it is built on is owned by the county. (Courtesy of Raul Medina III.)

Today, the AT&T Center is the new neighbor of the coliseum. The Stock Show and Rodeo still uses both facilities, but the majority of the events that come to San Antonio are held at the AT&T Center. The 18,500-seat center is home to the four-time NBA champion San Antonio Spurs. (Courtesy of Raul Medina III.)

Joske's was known for its elaborate Christmas decorations, which included holiday window displays and the elaborate fourth-floor Fantasyland, where children saw a winter forest, a miniature town square, and talking bears while standing in line with their parents to see Santa. The Saturday before Thanksgiving, Santa would arrive at the airport. He was greeted by Joske officials and driven to downtown on a fire engine. A welcoming party was held at Plaza de Valero, where the children received candy. Santa would climb the ladder to the roof and drop down a 25-foot chimney. A 30-foot mechanical replica of himself with a 6-foot mitten for waving was activated. The outdoor Santa enjoyed a commanding view of downtown San Antonio from the 1950s to the 1970s; while he was brought out of retirement in 1994, in 1997, he was severely damaged in a windstorm and permanently removed from the building's roof. Founded in 1867, Joske's closed in 1987 after the company was sold to Dillard's. Dillard's became the anchor store for Rivercenter Mall.

Today, the view from the Tower Life Building has not changed much. The only major addition was made during the 1980s, when Hyatt decided to build a hotel directly across from the Alamo. The hotel was planned to be a skyscraper, but fearing that the building would cast a shadow on the Alamo, the design of the hotel changed. In the future, this view may change with the River Walk Museum Reach Project as more downtown housing and offices are built. (Courtesy of Raul Medina III.)

The city is pictured in the 1950s during the Christmas holidays. The zigzagging street is Broadway. The 20-plus-story Nix Hospital was decorated with yellow lights, and the Christmas tree in Alamo Plaza can be seen in the upper right corner.

Three Brothers of Mary plus Brother Andrew Edel from the Society of Mary in Dayton, Ohio, built St. Mary's Institute as a private school for boys. It opened in 1853 and was known to San Antonians as the French School, although it offered other languages. The institute later became St. Mary's Academy and eventually became the downtown campus for St. Mary's University. (Courtesy of the Marianist Archives, San Antonio.)

When the school moved out to the west side of the city for a larger campus, Patrick J. Kennedy, a graduate of the law school, transformed the school into a hotel in time for the World's Fair in 1968. Today, the hotel is owned by Omni Hotels & Resorts and is the only AAA four-diamond hotel on the river. (Courtesy of Raul Medina III.)

This photograph shows Houston Street decorated with colorful lights during the holiday season in the early 1950s.

The photograph below shows the addition of trees along the sidewalk providing a canopy of lights in the present time. (Courtesy of David Peché.)

Holding one of his first postcards, here is author David L. Peché (right) sitting with his mother, who passed on a love of history. The lake grandstand and the Lone Star Pavilion are in the background.

Rick Peché was four, Mary Louise was 43, and author David L. Peché was seven when the first picture on the grounds of HemisFair Park was taken. The postcard the author holds is from the IBM Theater, which gave him his first understanding of computers. The lake is gone, and now a waterfall and water park has taken its place. (Courtesy of Raul Medina III.)

This photograph, taken in the late 1950s, shows a person carrying a stack of fruit baskets next to the Stein's store during the Battle of Flowers Parade. Author David L. Peché's family would take the bus downtown because it was easier than finding parking. Once there, the seat of choice were these baskets, as they only cost 25¢ a basket.

This Battle of the Flowers Parade photograph taken in 1959 has this well-dressed squad of girls turning left onto Houston Street. The colors on this orignal slide are blue and gold and could be those of the Alamo Heights Pep Squad.

Hoffmann & Hayman Coffee Company was located at 601 Delaware Street. Pictured is Manuel M. Peché, who at the age of 16 worked here before he was drafted into World War II. His duties where delivering coffee bags to businesses and helping to roast coffee beans. He also helped to offload coffee from the trains that traveled the tracks on the left side of the building. (Courtesy of Raul Medina III.)

Some 80-plus years later after the man on page 2 sat on the ledge looking at Alamo Plaza, Joan Marston Korte and David Peché revisit the spot. It has been an honor and a pleasure to share our passion of downtown San Antonio history. (Courtesy of Raul Medina III.)

Visit us at
arcadiapublishing.com

Printed in the USA
CPSIA information can be obtained
at www.ICGtesting.com
LVHW080325111023
760787LV00008B/52